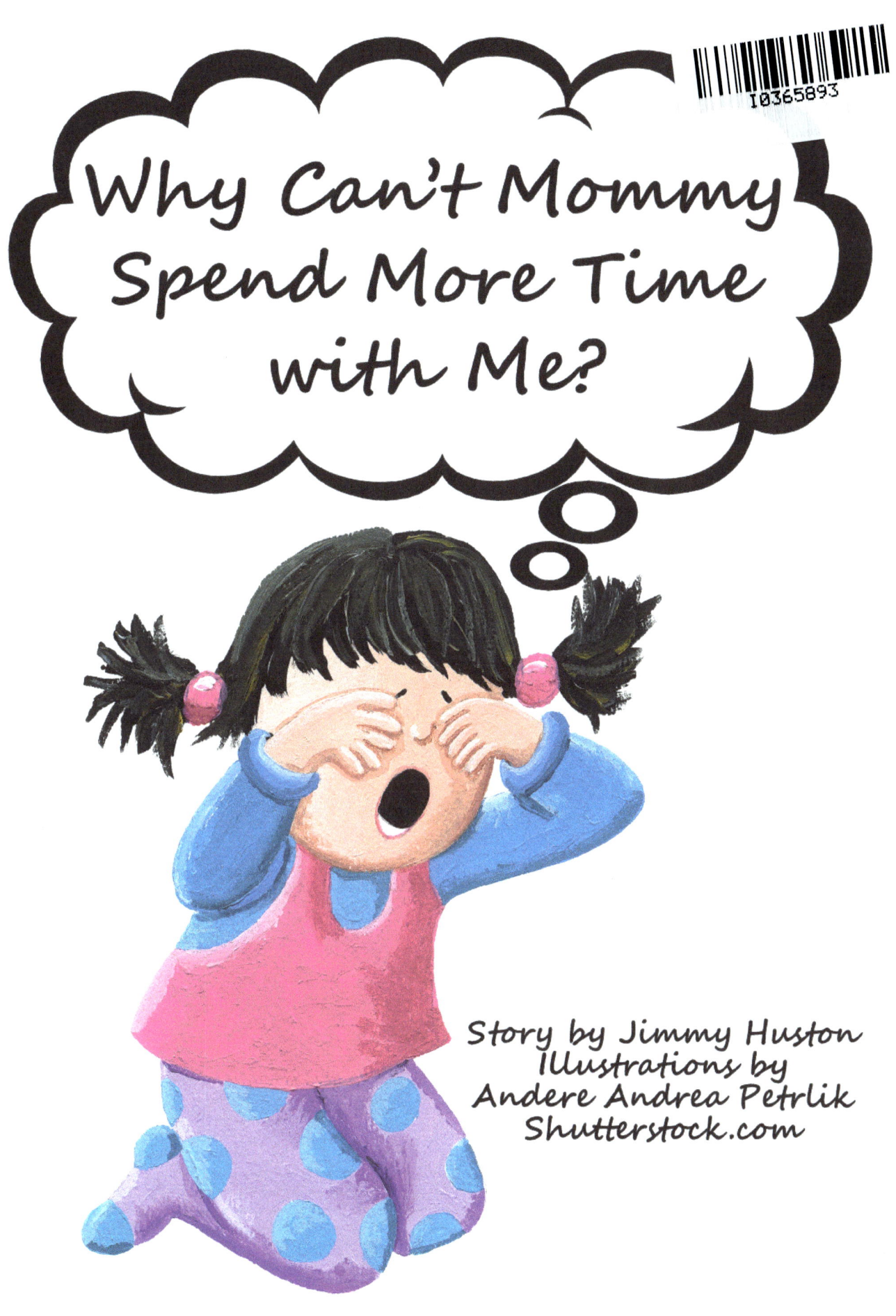

First Edition

Copyright © 2017 Jimmy Huston

ISBN: 978-1-970022-17-9

All rights reserved, including the right to use or reproduce this book or portions thereof in any form whatsoever without written permission from the publisher except in the case of brief quotations embodied in critical articles or reviews.

Andere Andrea Petrlik images are used under license from Shutterstock.com.

Cosworth Publishing
21545 Yucatan Avenue
Woodland Hills CA 91364
www.cosworthpublishing.com

For information regarding permission,
please send an email to office@cosworthpublishing.com.

Dedicated to your Mommy.

I have the best Mommy.

We've been together as long as I can remember.

She takes care of me
and makes me feel safe.

Mommy remembers my birthday.

She makes all the holidays special.

Mommy and I sing songs together.

Mommy plays games with me.

Mommy teaches me things.
She plays with me.
She takes me places.
She shows me everything.

Mommy does lots of stuff for me.

But then she gets busy.

She says she's run out of time, and doesn't have time to play.

Mommy always has time to cook.
I'm glad she does, because I can't cook and
I really like to eat.
I guess everybody does.

But she doesn't have time for me.

Mommy has time to clean the house.
That's nice, because it's good to live in a clean house.

But she doesn't have time for me.

Mommy has time to wash the dishes.
I'm glad she does, because I like my food on clean dishes.

But she doesn't have time for me.

Mommy has time to do the laundry.
She washes the clothes and she dries the clothes and she folds the clothes and she puts them away.
That's a good thing, because I like clean clothes.

But she doesn't have time for me.

Mommy has time to clean the house.
She has time to sweep the floor.
She has time to vacuum the carpet.
She has time to mop the kitchen.

But she doesn't have time for me.

Mommy has time to take out the garbage.
She has time to wash the windows.
She has time to scrub the bathroom.

But she doesn't have time for me.

Mommy has time to take me places.
That's good because I can't drive and I don't have a car.
I can learn to drive someday. But not yet.
So Mommy takes me lots of places.

But she doesn't have time for me.

Mommy has time to take me to school.
And she helps me with my homework when I need it.

And she works with me on my school projects, too.

But she doesn't have time for me.

When I don't feel well, Mommy takes care of me.

Sometimes she takes me to the doctor, even when she doesn't have time.

Okay, Mommy does a lot. I get it.
She does a lot for me.
And I guess I already know she could use some help --

-- so she would have some time for me.

I would help if I could.
But I can't cook.
I can't iron clothes, or sew.
And I can't drive.

I would help if I could, so Mommy would have time for me.

I can't cook, but I can wash an apple to eat.
I can make a sandwich.
I can make a salad.

So Mommy will have time for me.

With Mommy's help, there are things I can learn to make.
I can learn to make cereal.
I can learn to make toast.
I can learn to cook soup.
I can learn to cook pasta.

So Mommy will have time for me.

There are things I can't cook, but I can still help.
I can mix flour and water.
I can roll the dough.
I can lick the spoon.

So Mommy will have time for me.

I can set the table.
And I can clear the table.
I hate washing dishes, but I love spending time with Mommy, so --
-- I can wash the dishes and put them away.

So Mommy will have time for me.

I can clean my room.
I can pick up my dirty clothes.
I can pick up my toys.
I don't really want to do these things --

-- but I want to help Mommy.

I can sweep the floor.
I can straighten things in the house.
I can dust the things that I can reach.
I can fold my clothes and put them away.

So Mommy will have time for me.

Working hard is hard work.
And sometimes things go wrong.
It's okay to tell Mommy...
...I spilled the_____.
...I broke the_____.
...I yelled at_____.

Because Mommy loves me anyway.

I can play quietly by myself until Mommy has time for me.

I can read, or draw, or make up stories, or write songs and sing them to myself.

I know that Mommy loves to spend time with me.
Sometimes she just needs a little help.
I can do what I can to be her helper.

But most of all, I can say,
"Thank you, Mommy."

Like I said, "I have the best Mommy!"

We spend lots of time together.

I want to be just like her.

About Jimmy Huston

Jimmy Huston is a recovering screenwriter and filmmaker who has been distracted by his two daughters for the last twenty years and is finally getting back to work.

An escapee from Athens, Georgia, he is currently hiding in Woodland Hills, California.

jh@byjimmyhuston.com

Reviews are always appreciated.
(some more than others)

**Other Odd Little Books
by Jimmy Huston**

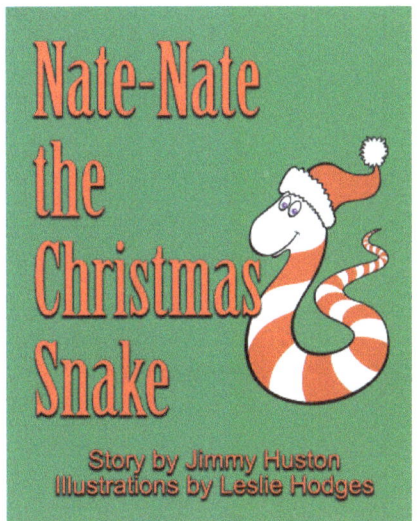
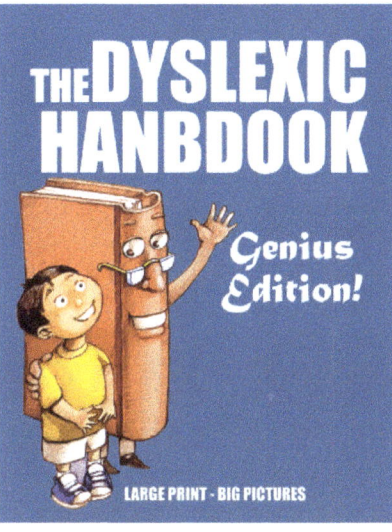
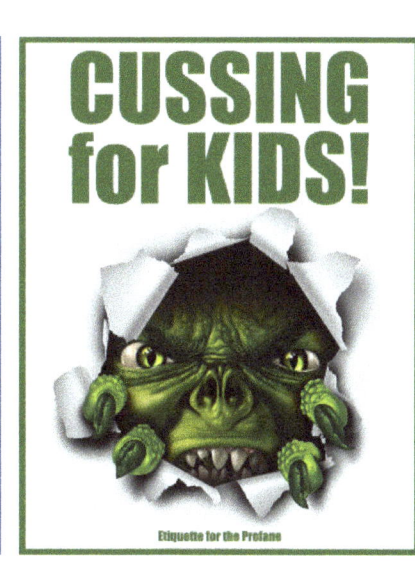

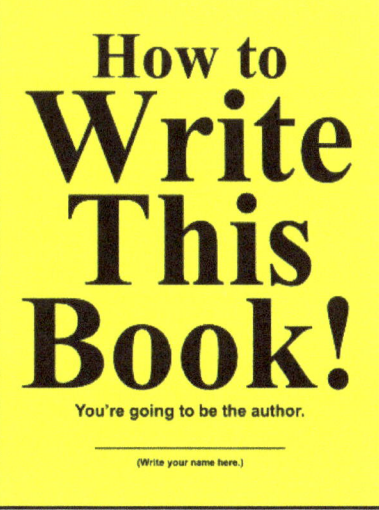

U-Draw books from Cosworth Publishing offer kids a chance to add their own creative artwork to illustrate these books.
www.udrawbooks.com

Send us some of your art and we'll put it on our websites.

Other books from Cosworth Publishing
www.cosworthpublishing.com

Find it wherever good books are dreaded.

If you're reading this, you will not like this book. It's not for you.

This book is for all the people who are not reading this.

They won't like it either, but it's short.

They'll like that.

"I didn't actually read this book. If I had, I would have loved it — but I never will."
                     Billy

" 'Hate' isn't a strong enough word for me. I loathe reading. I don't even like looking at pictures — which there are none of."
                     Wally

"This isn't what I wrote about this stupid book."
                     Zane

"This is an excellent coffee table book, if your coffee table hates to read."
                    Solomon

"This book made my teacher cry."   David

"My son loved this book. He said it was delicious."
                    Mr. Jones

"THIS BOOK IS SO DUMB THAT I COULD'VE WRITTEN IT."
                     Jimmy

www.i-hate-to-read.com

One of the very best new books about Christmas and reptiles!

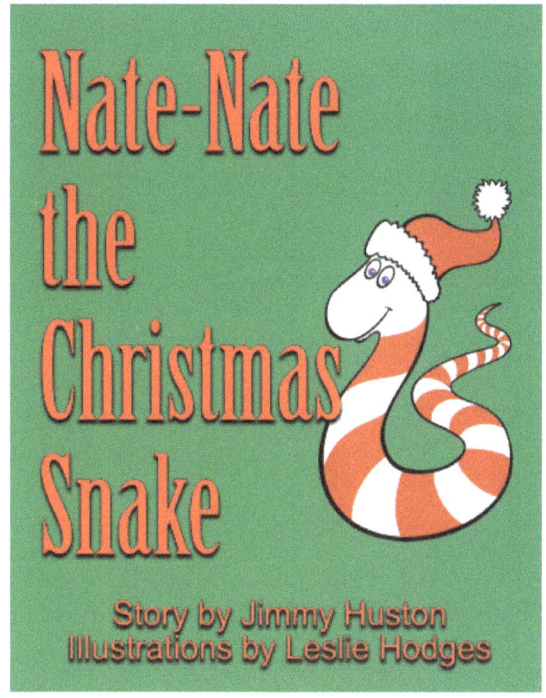

Ripped from the headlines of Candy Cane Lane!

Follow little Nate-Nate as he explores Candy Cane Lane on Christmas Eve. He is not exactly welcomed by the neighborhood, but through his adventures Nate-Nate discovers the spirit of Christmas despite being a lowly snake in everyone's eyes.

When the joyful holiday mood is threatened, he slithers to the rescue and becomes the legend known far and wide as Nate-Nate the Christmas Snake.

NOW AVAILABLE AS AN AUDIOBOOK ON AUDIBLE.COM
Read by Sean Philip Glasgow

No snakes were harmed in the writing of this book.

www.christmassnake.com

Dead Is the New Sick
An Insider's Guide to Senility, Paranoia, & Curmudgery

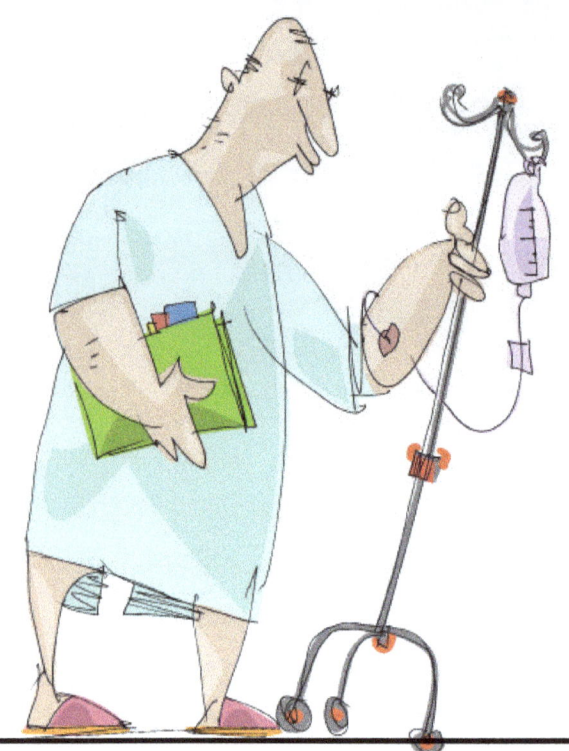

"Warmly affectionate elder abuse." — Methuselah

"Sadly funny..." — Sophocles

"The Pet Rock of western literature." — Anon.

"I don't feel so good." — John Doe

Top 10 Warnings

1. Hospice is a crock. Keep a jug of water under the bed.
2. Write a will.
4. Hide it.
5. Don't walk toward the light.
6. Did you take your meds today?
7. Are you sure?
8. What happened to Number 3?
9. Eat a pie.
10. If there has ever been something you wanted to do, but didn't for whatever reason, now is the time to do it! Start with this book!

www.deadsick.com

Books for Grownups from Cosworth Publishing
www.cosworthpublishing.com

A semi-serious treatise argues college is more expensive than travel to Europe, suggesting an extended stay abroad could be more enlightening than higher education.

A humorous compendium of ill-conceived advice and misunderstood life-lessons provide affectionate elder abuse. A great birthday gift.

As World War II erupts, a young Jewish scribe flees Lithuania with his in-progress Torah, meeting Chinese calligraphers while living under Japanese occupation.

A practical guide for the person who is confronted by the possibile suicide of a friend or family member.

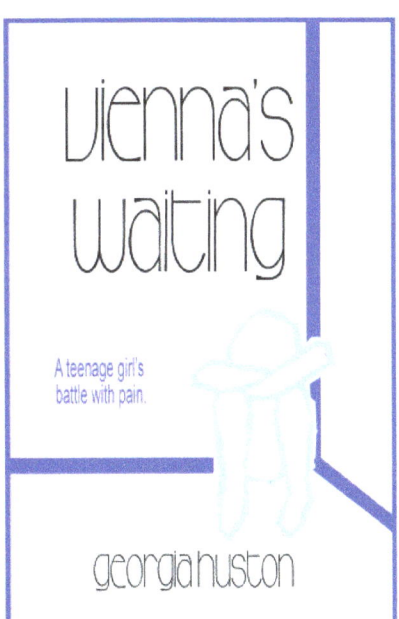

At 14, Georgia developed mysterious chronic pain. This book chronicles that dark time and follows her inspirational journey back to health and happiness.

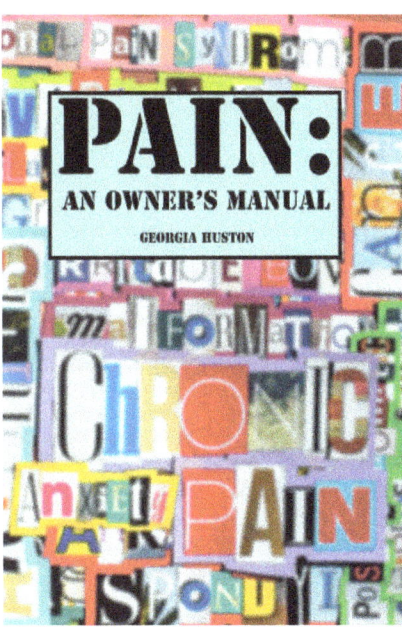

A young pain victim's inspirational and informative conversations with a variety of pain sufferers and specialists. Doctors should read this at their own risk.

www.ingramcontent.com/pod-product-compliance
Lightning Source LLC
Chambersburg PA
CBHW040004080526
44586CB00027B/2877